The Awakening of Universal Motherhood

Sri Mata Amritanandamayi Devi

The Awakening of Universal Motherhood

An address given by
Sri Mata Amritanandamayi Devi

at the
Global Peace Initiative of Women
Religious and Spiritual Leaders.

Palais des Nations, Geneva
October 7th, 2002

Mata Amritanandamayi Mission Trust
Amritapuri P.O., Kollam 690 525, Kerala, India

The Awakening of Universal Motherhood

Published by:
Mata Amritanandamayi Mission Trust
Amritapuri PO, Kollam Dt., Kerala, India 690 525
E-mail: inform@amritapuri.org
Website: www.amritapuri.org
Phone: (0476) 2896278, 2897578, 2896179,
2896399

Copyright © 2012 by Mata Amritanandamayi Mission Trust

All rights reserved. No part of this publication may be stored in a retrieval system, transmitted, reproduced, transcribed or translated into any language, in any form, by any means without the prior agreement and written permission of the publisher.

Second Edition: September 2004, 2000 copies
Sixth printing: June 2012, 1000 copies
Seventh printing: June 2013
Typesetting and layout: Amrita DTP, Amritapuri

Contents

Foreword 9

Acceptance Speech 29

Keynote Address 33

Prayer

ॐ

असतो मा सद्गमय

तमसो मा ज्योतिर्गमय

मृत्योर्मा अमृतं गमय

ॐ शान्तिः शान्तिः शान्तिः

Om

asato mā sadgamaya

tamaso mā jyotirgamaya

mṛtyormā amṛtaṁ gamaya

Om śāntiḥ śāntiḥ śāntiḥ

Om
Lead us from untruth to Truth,
from darkness to Light,
from death to Immortality.
Om, peace, peace, peace.

With the Light of Peace

Foreword

THE POWER OF MOTHERHOOD

By Swami Amritaswarupananda Puri

When the nations of the world, shocked by the bloodshed and conflict caused by the First World War, joined hands, a temple of peace arose: the League of Nations. Its headquarters were in Geneva, Switzerland. At a time when nations were competing to show who was mightier, the League was a lamp showing the ruling classes and ordinary people the way to peace—that was its aim. Even though the Second World War put an end to the League of Nations, the nations of the world came together again; and this gathering led to the formation of the United Nations.

From October 6th to 9th, 2002, there was another coming together of nations in Geneva: a meeting of women religious and spiritual leaders from all parts of the world and all religions, organized by the Global Peace Initiative of Women Religious and Spiritual Leaders. This conference was an initiative of The Millennium World Peace Summit held two years earlier at the United Nations in New York.

Representatives from about 125 nations participated in the Geneva Initiative.

On October 6th, there were two main sessions: The first was held in the Hotel Beau-Rivage, in the heart of Geneva. The women gathered as one community transcending boundaries of religion, culture, race, and language. United in their sincere yearning for global peace, they prayed and meditated together—a first step on the path to peace.

At about three o'clock, Amma arrived at the entrance of the Hotel Beau-Rivage. The Convener of the Global Peace Initiative, Ms. Dena Merriam, and the Secretary-General of The Millennium World Peace Summit, Mr. Bawa Jain, were waiting in the foyer to receive Her. They escorted Amma to meet with representatives of the Ruder Finn Group and an American documentary-making company, One Voice International, who immediately engaged her in interviews.

"If at all there is a way to global peace, what is it?" This question was from the Ruder Finn Group.

Amma smiled, "That is very simple. First, change should take place within. Then, the world will change automatically—and peace will prevail."

Question: "What kind of change?"

Amma: "Changes caused by imbibing the spiritual principles."

One Voice International then asked Amma, "What can be done to change the mentality of men and society, which regard women as subordinate?"

"A woman should abide firmly in motherhood, which is intrinsic to her." Amma's response was so natural to her.

Question: "Is Amma saying that woman should not venture into other spheres of society?

Amma: "No, Amma is saying that woman should venture into all spheres of society. But, whatever she does, she should have firm faith in the power of motherhood. Actions devoid of that, in any sphere, will not help women to progress, but will weaken them."

Amma was, in this exchange, foreshadowing the speech she would deliver the next day at the Palais des Nations. There, she would explain that "Motherhood" is a quality that men and women alike can—indeed, should—develop:

> The love of awakened motherhood is a love and compassion felt not only towards one's own children, but towards all people, animals and plants, rocks and rivers—a love extended to all of nature, to all beings. Indeed, to a woman in whom the state of true motherhood has awakened, all creatures are her children.

This love, this motherhood, is Divine Love—and that is God.

The interview continued:

Question: "What is Amma's opinion about men's attitude in general?"

Amma: "They are also Amma's children. But, even now, they find it hard to internalize the respect and recognition that they show outwardly to their wife, mother or sister. Generally, they believe more in muscle power!"

This Global Initiative for peace was held not quite one year after the devastating terrorist acts of September 11. So it was fitting that the next event that first afternoon harkened back to those terrible times. Ms. Debra Olsen of One Voice International introduced an American woman fire fighter to Amma. Ms. Olsen said, "This is Jennifer. She has come from New York. She was present at the World Trade Center on the day of the terrorist attack, to help extinguish the fire. She still has not fully recovered from the shock of that disaster. Amma should bless her."

Perhaps Amma was thinking about the plight of the thousands of helpless and innocent people who died that day, for her face and eyes clearly reflected sorrow. While Amma was lovingly hugging

Jennifer and wiping away her tears, tears welled up in Amma's eyes, too. Tears also filled the eyes of many of those who witnessed this heart-moving scene.

Jennifer had brought something strange from the site of the World Trade Center, now known as "Ground Zero." It appeared to be a chunk of concrete and a key, melted in the inferno of the devastating fire. Showing them to Amma, she said, "I'm not sure why I brought them, but I needed to bring the pain with me. And I was hoping to bring these home feeling something different. I've come here with so much anger, in the hope of having some peace in my heart." Saying so, she offered the terrible mementos to Amma. Amma respectfully received them and, bringing them to Her face, kissed them.

Debra Olsen then asked Amma, "Jennifer has no belief in God or in any religion. But she has love and compassion towards the suffering. Is there any need for her to pray to any God?"

Amma replied, "God is love and compassion towards the suffering. If one has such a heart, there is no need to pray to God."

Many other questions were asked. Beautifully simple answers flowed from Amma.

When the interview with Jennifer was over, the

famous Hollywood actress Linda Evans came to meet Amma. She was overjoyed to see Amma. "I have heard so much about you. It is only now that I have been able to meet you. What a blessing!" said Ms. Evans.

She gazed at Amma for some time. Then she asked, "What is the purpose of divine motherhood?"

Amma: "It is an attitude of the mind—expansiveness."

Ms. Evans: "How do we gain that?"

Amma: "It is not different from us. Neither is it something to be gained from without. That power is within. When you realize this, universal motherhood will spontaneously awaken in you."

At this point, Mother was escorted to another room where she was to meet the previous year's recipient of the Gandhi-King Award, the woman who would be handing that award to Amma the next morning: the world-famous primatologist, Dr. Jane Goodall. There was an immediate and deep resonance between the two of them. It seemed as if Dr. Goodall could not get enough, no matter how many hugs she received from Amma. She said, "You are so sweet, beyond words!" After a pause, she added, "Beyond compare also."

Dr. Goodall, who spent 20 years in African

jungles with animals, especially chimpanzees, to study and to understand their minds, then asked Amma, "What is your opinion about animals being able to understand the hearts of human beings, and thus respond to them?"

Amma: "Animals can certainly understand human hearts and act accordingly, perhaps better than humans themselves. Amma has personally experienced this."

Amma then shared with Dr. Goodall some of Her own experiences during the years she spent with nature and animals. Amma talked about the dog that brought her food packets, the eagle that dropped raw fish in her lap, the cow that emerged from the cowshed and stood in front of her in such a way as to allow Amma to drink directly from her udders, the parrot that shed tears when Amma tearfully sang bhajans, and the doves that danced before Amma while she sang.

After her conversation with Dr. Goodall, Amma met and embraced the other people in the room: Bawa Jain, Dena Merriam, Cambodian princess Ratna Devi Noordam, and the Peace Initiative's co-chair the Reverend Joan Campbell. Then it was time to join the prayer session being held in the hotel ballroom.

Amma led the prayer for world peace, chanting

three times, *"Lokah samastah sukhino bhavantu* [May all beings in all the worlds be happy]." Everyone repeated the mantra after Amma. Before the waves of the peace mantra had subsided, Amma began the "Ma-Om" meditation, guiding and sustaining the delegates in that practice for ten minutes. By the time she ended the prayer with Sri Shankaracharya's *Nirvanashtakam*, many delegates from different nations could feel the blessing of peace pulsating within.

The second main event of the day was the convening of all the conference participants at the English Garden Lake Park. Upon her arrival, Amma was introduced and stepped to the podium. In her peace message, Amma said, "What everyone needs is peace. But a majority want to be king. No one wants to be a servant. How can there be peace then? Won't there only be war and conflict? A true servant is the real king. Isn't the milk from the black cow, the white cow, and the brown cow always white? Similarly, the essence in every person is the same. Peace and contentment are the same for everyone. Those who desire these should work together." When Amma and a number of other delegates to the Peace Initiative had finished their talks, all the delegates chanted in unison, "We do not want war at all. We do not want crime. We want only peace!" The delegates lit candles and held them aloft to symbolize the light of peace that removes the darkness of war and conflict. Holding their candles high, the participants, speakers, and audience members then arranged themselves on the lawn to form the letters of the word "P-E-A-C-E." So many people wanted to stay close to Amma that the photographers (from a nearby rooftop) finally decided to add an exclamation point after the word "peace" since Amma and the group huddled around Her naturally formed a point!

The next day was October 7th, the day of the Initiative's main session. When Amma reached the United Nations assembly hall at 9:00 a.m., Bawa Jain and Dena Merriam were on hand to welcome her. The hall was packed with spiritual leaders and preceptors representing various religions.

One after the other spoke on women's liberty and the social problems women face. The profound limitations women are forced to experience, proposed solutions, and advice were eloquently articulated and analyzed, without the unnecessary criticism or undercurrents of egotism that so often emerge at some events.

A woman and her motherhood are not two; that they are one was proved by the sense of purity that prevailed in the atmosphere. The humility of the organizers and the clockwork-precision with which the day's programs unfolded were especially noteworthy.

At 11:00 a.m., women religious and spiritual leaders from the Philippines, Thailand, Israel, China, Afghanistan, and Rwanda spoke very briefly yet passionately on "Women and Their Contributions to World Peace." Thereafter, Ms. Susan Deihim from Iran expressed, through a song, the global longing for peace.

At 11:20 a.m., Dena Merriam arrived on the podium. Looking at the audience, she smiled, and said, "Next is the most important ceremony of this event: the presentation of this year's Gandhi-King Award for Non-violence. I respectfully call upon Sri Mata Amritanandamayi Devi to come up on stage to accept the award."

The audience clapped enthusiastically and rose to give a standing ovation as Amma, with her characteristic humility and simplicity, rose from her seat, walked up the steps onto the stage, and proceeded towards the dignitaries awaiting her, folding her hands in the traditional Indian gesture of respect and reverence towards the divinity in all.

The United Nations' Human Rights High Commissioner, His Excellency Sergio Vieira de

Mello, greeted Amma and ushered Her onto the stage. Bawa Jain introduced him to Amma. In her usual style, Amma hugged him and affectionately kissed his hand. The Commissioner reciprocated by affectionately kissing both of Amma's hands.

For the next few minutes, Bawa Jain addressed the assembly, recalling the previous recipients of the Gandhi-King Award: Kofi Annan (in 1999), Nelson Mandela (in 2000) and Jane Goodall (in 2001). He then invited Dr. Goodall to introduce Amma to the assembly and present the award to her. Dr. Goodall spoke from her heart:

> I feel it's a great honour to share a platform with a woman who is so remarkable, and who is the very embodiment of goodness. She's had a remarkable life. She has defied tradition from the beginning. Born to a poor family, with her skin darker than those of her brothers and sisters, she was not treated well by her family; she was treated as a servant. But she began to feel the presence of God within her, and so powerfully did she feel that presence, that she wanted to reach out and share her good fortune with those who were less fortunate than she. And again defying tradition, she began to embrace those who were in need of comfort, when women were not supposed to

touch strangers. And she has comforted with her wonderful hugging, which I experienced yesterday, more than 21 million people—think of it: 21 million people! But more than that, she has established a vast network of charitable organizations, ranging from schools and hospitals, and orphanages, and building homes for the poor—too many to mention here. And finally, again defying tradition, she was the first religious leader to invest women as priests in the traditional temples. She believes that God does not discriminate between the sexes, and I believe that she stands here in front of us, God's love in a human body.

When Dr. Goodall proceeded to present the 2002 Gandhi-King Award to Amma, there was a tremendous outpouring of emotion. The delegates rose to their feet, clapping and cheering.

When the applause drew to a close, Bawa Jain invited Amma to speak on the subject of "The Power of Motherhood." Amma chose to first say a few words in acknowledgement of the award for non-violence that she had just received. She began by acknowledging Mahatma Gandhi and Dr. Martin Luther King, Jr., saying that those two peace advocates had been able to achieve great successes because they had purity of heart and the strength of popular support. Amma spoke of those who strive for world peace and contentment for all, saying that it is such people who deserve this award, and that she was accepting it on their behalf. Amma also prayed that those who work for world peace would be blessed with more strength and courage. Amma reminded the delegates:

> Mahatma Gandhi and the Reverend Martin Luther King dreamt of a world in which human beings are recognized and loved as human beings, without prejudice of any kind. Remembering them, Amma also places a vision of the future before you. It is a vision of a world in which women and men progress together, a world in which all men respect the fact that, like the two wings of a bird, women and men are of equal value. For without the two in perfect balance, humanity cannot progress.

With these words, Amma moved on to her keynote speech:

> Women and men are equal in Amma's eyes. Amma wants to honestly express Her views on this very subject. These observations don't necessarily apply to everyone, but they do

apply to the majority of people. Women have to wake up and arise! At present, most women are asleep. The awakening of the dormant power of women is one of the most urgent needs of the age.

Fundamental truths flowed from Amma for the next twenty minutes. The inner and outer nature of women; the depth, range and self-imposed limitations of women's minds; the ways in which cultural realities and attitudes have held women down; the infinite power latent within women... as Amma addressed all these issues with compelling clarity and insight, the assembly listened in silence, reflective and attentive. In those moments, the sheer power of Amma's words and the presence of her universal motherhood were palpable.

By the end of the speech, Amma had made it clear that this "universal motherhood" was a quality all people should seek to develop—men as well as women:

> The essence of motherhood is not restricted to women who have given birth; it is a principle inherent in both women and men. It is an attitude of the mind. It is love — and that love is the very breath of life. No one would say, 'I will breathe only when I am with my

family and friends; I won't breathe in front of my enemies.' Similarly, for those in whom motherhood has awakened, love and compassion towards everyone is as much part of their being as breathing.

Amma feels that the forthcoming age should be dedicated to re-awakening the healing power of motherhood. This is the only way to realize our dream of peace and harmony for all.

When Amma concluded her speech, the assembly spontaneously stood up, applauding resoundingly.

After the session had ended, a good number of the participants rushed up to the great wonder that is Amma, to look at her, to meet her and to receive her darshan. Meanwhile, in another part of the hall, there was a mad rush to get a copy of Amma's speech.

Amidst all this, Bawa Jain arrived, requesting Amma to attend a photo session with the other delegates. People began trailing Amma wherever she went, like bees after the queen bee. Mr. Jain had a hard time getting to Amma through the thick crowds pressing around her. Finally, he said to those around Amma, "Hey, she is also my Mother. Give me a chance, too!"

Accompanied by the Reverend Joan Campbell, Dr. Goodall, the Cambodian princess, Ratna Devi Noordam, Bawa Jain and Dena Merriam, Amma left the assembly hall and went outside. On the veranda in front of the hall, the co-chair of the Global Peace Initiative for Women Religious and Spiritual Leaders, Dr. Saleha Mahmood Abedin, a woman from Pakistan, was waiting to meet Amma. As soon as she saw Amma, Dr. Abedin, an Islamic scholar and socialist, went up to Amma and greeted her. Amma embraced her with great love. As she stood with her head on Amma's shoulder, Dr. Abedin said softly, "It is such a great blessing that you are here with us today."

Following the photo session, the Christian Broadcasting Corporation requested an interview.

Question: "Amma receives people by hugging them. Can this hug help one attain peace?"

Amma: "It is not a mere hug, but one that awakens the spiritual principles. Our essence is love. We live for love, don't we? Where there is love, there is no conflict, only peace."

Question: "Amma has followers all over the world. Do they all worship you?"

Amma: "Amma worships *them*. All of them

are my God. Amma does not have a God who dwells beyond the skies. My God is all of you, everything that can be seen. Amma loves everyone and everything, and they love me as much. Love flows both ways. There, there is no duality, only oneness—pure love."

Indeed, this is the secret of this great being who attracts the whole world to Herself—this is the never-ceasing flow of the River of Love—the power of an indescribable universal motherhood.

Swami Amritaswarupananda
Amritapuri, Kerala

Global Peace Initiative of Women Religious and Spiritual Leaders.

*Palais des Nations, Genève.
October 7th, 2002*

This award has been instituted in fond remembrance of two great personalities—Mahatma Gandhi and Reverend Martin Luther King. Amma's prayer on this occasion is that all those people who pray and work for peace all over the world will gain more strength and inspiration, and that more and more people will work for world peace. Amma is receiving this award on their behalf. Amma's life has been offered to the world, so She doesn't make any claims.

– Amma

Acceptance Speech

*Delivered upon receiving the 2002
Gandhi-King Award for Non-violence*

Amma bows down to all of you, who are truly the embodiments of supreme love and pure consciousness.

This award has been instituted in fond remembrance of two great personalities—Mahatma Gandhi and Reverend Martin Luther King. Amma's prayer on this occasion is that all those people who pray and work for peace all over the world will gain more strength and inspiration, and that more and more people will work for world peace. Amma is receiving this award on their behalf. Amma's life has been offered to the world, so She doesn't make any claims.

Both Mahatma Gandhi and Reverend Martin Luther King dreamt of a world in which human beings are recognized and loved as human beings, without prejudice of any kind. Remembering them, Amma also places a vision of the future before you.

Amma, too, has a dream. It is a vision of a world in which women and men progress together, a world in which all men respect the fact that, like

the two wings of a bird, women and men are of equal value. For without the two in perfect balance, humanity cannot progress.

Dr. King was courageous like a lion, yet in his heart he was as soft as a flower. He risked his life for the sake of love, equality, and the other noble ideals he upheld. He had to struggle with great perseverance against the people of his own country.

And Mahatma Gandhi didn't just preach. He put his words into action. He dedicated his whole life to peace and non-violence. Even though he could have become the prime minister or president of India, Gandhi declined because he had no desire whatsoever for fame or power. In fact, at the stroke of midnight, when India was declared independent, Gandhi was found consoling the victims of a riot-affected area.

It is easy to awaken someone who is asleep. You just shake the person once or twice. But you can shake a person who is pretending to be asleep a hundred times and it won't have any effect. The majority of people belong to the latter category. It is high time that we all truly wake up. Unless the baser animal tendencies in people are subdued, our vision for the future of humanity will not come true, and peace will remain only a distant dream.

Let us have the courage and perseverance, born out of spiritual practice, to realize this dream. For this to happen, each one of us needs to discover and bring to light our innate qualities of faith, love, patience, and self-sacrifice for the good of all. This is what Amma calls true motherhood.

Keynote Address

THE AWAKENING OF UNIVERSAL MOTHERHOOD

By Sri Mata Amritanandamayi Devi

Amma's address on the occasion of A Global Peace Initiative of Women Religious and Spiritual Leaders, Palais des Nations, Geneva, 7 October, 2002

Amma bows down to all of you who are truly the embodiments of supreme consciousness and love.

Women and men are equal in Amma's eyes. Amma wants to honestly express her views on this very subject. These observations don't necessarily apply to everyone, but they do apply to the majority of people.

At present, most women are asleep. Women have to wake up and arise! This is one of the most urgent needs of the age. Not only should women living in developing countries wake up—this applies to women all over the world. Women in countries where materialism is predominant should awaken to spirituality[1]. And women in countries where they are forced to remain inside the narrow walls of religious tradition should awaken to modern thinking. It has been widely believed that women and the cultures in which they live will awaken through education and material development. But time has taught us that this concept is too limited. Only when women imbibe the eternal wisdom of spirituality, along with modern education, will the power within them awaken—and they will rise to action.

Who should awaken woman? What obstructs her awakening? In truth, no external power can possibly obstruct woman or her innate qualities of motherhood—qualities such as love, empathy, and patience. It is she—she alone—who has to awaken herself. A woman's mind is the only real barrier that prevents this from happening.

---

[1] The spirituality that Amma refers to here is not about worshipping a God sitting somewhere up above the clouds. Real spirituality is to know oneself and to realize the infinite Power within. Spirituality and life are not two separate things; they are one. Real spirituality teaches us how to live in the world. Material science teaches us how to air-condition the external world, whereas spiritual science teaches us how to "air-condition" the internal world.

The rules and superstitious beliefs that degrade women continue to prevail in most countries. The primitive customs invented by men in the past to exploit and to subjugate women remain alive to this day. Women and their minds have become entangled in the cobweb of those customs. They have been hypnotized by their own minds. Women have to help themselves in order to extricate themselves from that magnetic field. This is the only way.

Look at an elephant. It can uproot huge trees with its trunk. When an elephant living in captivity is still a baby, it is tied to a tree with a strong rope or a chain. Because it is the nature of elephants to roam free, the baby elephant instinctively tries with all its might to break the rope. But it isn't strong enough to do so. Realizing its efforts are of no use, it finally gives up and stops struggling. Later, when the elephant is fully grown, it can be tied to a small tree with a thin rope. It could then easily free itself by uprooting the tree or breaking the rope. But because its mind has been conditioned by its prior experiences, it doesn't make the slightest attempt to break free.

This is what is happening to women. Society does not allow the strength of women to arise. We have created a blockage, preventing this great strength from flowing out.

The infinite potential inherent in women and men is the same. If women really want to, it won't be difficult to break the shackles—the rules and conditioning that society has imposed on them. The greatest strength of women lies in their innate motherhood, in their creative, life-giving power. And this power can help women to bring about a far more significant change in society than men could ever accomplish.

Antiquated, crippling concepts devised in the past are blocking women from reaching spiritual heights. Those are the shadows that still haunt women, evoking fear and distrust within. Women should let go of their fear and distrust—they are simply illusions. The limitations women think they have are not real. Women need to muster the strength to overcome those imagined limitations. They already possess this power; it is right here! And once that power has been evoked, no one will be able to stop the forward march of women in every area of life.

Men normally believe in muscle power. On a superficial level they see women as their mothers, wives, and sisters. But there is no need to hide the fact that, on a deeper level, men still have a great deal of resistance when it comes to properly understanding, accepting, and recognizing women and the feminine aspect of life.

Amma remembers a story. In a village there lived a deeply spiritual woman who found immense happiness in serving others. The religious leaders of the village chose her as one of their priests. She was the first appointed woman priest in the area, and the male priests didn't like it one bit. Her great compassion, humility, and wisdom were appreciated by the villagers. This caused a lot of jealousy among the male priests.

One day all the priests were invited to a religious gathering on an island, three hours away by boat. As the priests boarded the boat they discovered, to their dismay, that the woman priest was already seated inside. They muttered among themselves, "What a pain! She just won't leave us alone!" The boat set off. But an hour later the engine suddenly died and the boat came to a standstill. The captain exclaimed, "Oh, no! We're stuck! I forgot to fill the tank!" Nobody knew what to do. There was no other boat in sight. At this point the woman priest stood up and said, "Don't worry, brothers! I'll go and fetch more fuel." Having said this, she stepped out of the boat and proceeded to walk away across the water. The priests watched with great astonishment, but were quick to remark, "Look at her! She doesn't even know how to swim!"

This is the attitude of men in general. It lies in their nature to belittle and condemn the achievements of women. Women are not decorations or objects meant to be controlled by men. Men treat women like potted plants, making it impossible for them to grow to their full potential.

Women were not created for the enjoyment of men. They were not made to host tea parties. Men use women like a tape recorder, which they like to control according to their whims and fancies, as if they were pressing play and pause buttons.

Men consider themselves superior to women, both physically and intellectually. The arrogance of men's mistaken attitude—that women cannot survive in society without depending on men—is obvious in everything that men do.

If a woman's character is considered flawed, even if she is an innocent victim, she will be rejected by society and often by her family. Whereas, a man can be as immoral as he likes and get away with it. He is seldom questioned.

Even in materially developed countries, women are pushed back when it comes to sharing political power with men. It is interesting to see that, compared to developed countries, developing countries are far ahead in providing opportunities for women to rise in politics. But, except for a few who can be counted on one's fingers, how many women can be seen in the arena of world politics? Is it this way because women are incapable, or is it due to the arrogance of men?

The right circumstances and support of others will certainly help women to awaken and arise. But this alone is not enough. They need to draw inspiration from those circumstances and find strength within themselves. Real power and strength do not come from the outside; they are to be found within.

Women have to find their courage. Courage is an attribute of the mind; it is not a quality of the body. Women have the power to fight against the social rules that prevent their progress. This is Amma's own experience. Though a lot of changes have taken place, India is a country where male supremacy is still the rule. Even today, women are exploited in the name of religious convention and tradition. In India, too, women are waking up and springing into action. Until recently, women were not allowed to worship in the inner sanctum of a temple; nor could women consecrate a temple or perform Vedic rituals. Women didn't even have the freedom to chant Vedic mantras. But Amma is encouraging and appointing women to do these things. And it is Amma who performs the consecration ceremony in all the temples built by our ashram. There were many who protested against women doing these things, because for generations all those ceremonies and rituals had been done only by men. To those who questioned what we were doing, Amma explained that we are worshipping a God who is beyond all differences, who does not differentiate between male and female. As it turns out, the majority of people have supported this revolutionary move. Those prohibitions against women were never actually a part of ancient Hindu tradition. They were in all likelihood invented later by men who belonged to the higher classes of society, in order to exploit and oppress women. They didn't exist in ancient India.

In ancient India, the Sanskrit words that a husband used when addressing his wife were *Pathni*—the one who leads the husband through life; *Dharmapathni*—the one who guides her husband on the path of *dharma* [righteousness and responsibility]; and *Sahadharmacharini*—the one who moves together with her husband on the path of *dharma*. These terms imply that women enjoyed the same status as men, or perhaps an even higher one. Married life was considered sacred; for if lived with the right attitude and right understanding, with both husband and wife supporting each other, it would lead them to the ultimate goal of life—Self-realization or God-realization.

In India, the Supreme Being has never been worshipped exclusively in a masculine form. The Supreme Being is also worshipped as the Goddess in Her many aspects. She is, for example, worshipped as Saraswati, the Goddess of wisdom and learning; She is worshipped as Lakshmi, the Goddess of prosperity; and Santana Lakshmi, the Goddess who gives new life within a woman. She is also worshipped as Durga, the Goddess of strength and power. There was a time when men revered woman as the embodiment of these very qualities. She was considered an extension of the Goddess, a manifestation of Her attributes on Earth. And then, at some point, because of the selfishness of certain men of influence and their desire for power and dominion over all, this deep truth was distorted and severed from our culture. And thus it was that people forgot or ignored the profound connection between woman and the Divine Mother.

It is commonly believed that the religion that gives least status to women is Islam. But the Koran speaks of qualities such as compassion and wisdom, and of God's essential nature, as feminine.

In Christianity, the Supreme Being is worshipped

exclusively as the Father in Heaven, the Son, and the Holy Ghost. The feminine aspect of God is not so widely recognized. Christ considered men and women equal.

For Christ, Krishna, and Buddha to be born, a woman was needed. In order to incarnate, God needed a woman, who went through all the pain and hardship of pregnancy and giving birth. A man was not capable of this. Yet no one considers the injustice of women being ruled by men. No genuine religion will look down upon women or speak of women in a derogatory manner.

For those who have realized God, there is no difference between male and female. The realized ones have equal vision. If anywhere in the world there exist rules that prevent women from enjoying their rightful freedom, rules that obstruct their progress in society, then those are not God's commandments, but are born out of the selfishness of men.

Which eye is more important, the left or the right? Both are equally important. It is the same with the status of men and women in society. Both should be aware of their unique responsibilities, or *dharma*. Men and women have to support one another. Only in this way can we maintain the harmony of the world. When men and women become powers that complement each other, and move together with cooperation and mutual respect, they will attain perfection.

In reality, men are a part of women. Every child first lies in the mother's womb, as a part of the woman's very being. As far as a birth is concerned, a man's only role is to offer his seed. For him it is only a moment of pleasure; for a woman it is nine months of austerities. It is the woman who receives, conceives, and makes that life a part of her being. She creates the most conducive atmosphere for that life to grow within her and then gives birth to that life. Women are essentially mothers, the creators of life. There is a hidden longing in all men to be re-enfolded by the unconditional love of a mother. This is one of the subtle reasons for the attraction that men feel towards women—because a man is born out of a woman.

No one can question the reality of motherhood—that men are created from women. Yet those who refuse to come out of the cocoon of their narrow minds will never be able to understand. You cannot explain light to those who know only darkness.

The principle of motherhood is as vast and powerful as the universe. With the power of motherhood within her, a woman can influence the entire world.

Universal Motherhood

Is God a man or a woman? The answer to that question is that God is neither male nor female—God is "That." But if you insist on God having a gender, then God is more female than male, because the masculine is contained within the feminine.

Anyone—woman or man—who has the courage to overcome the limitations of the mind can attain the state of universal motherhood. The love of awakened motherhood is a love and compassion felt not only towards one's own children, but towards all people, animals and plants, rocks and rivers—a love extended to all of nature, all beings. Indeed, to a woman in whom the state of true motherhood has awakened, all creatures are her children. This love, this motherhood, is Divine Love—and that is God.

More than half of the world's population are women. It is a great loss when women are denied the freedom to come forward, and when they are denied the high status that should be theirs in society. When women are denied this, society loses their potential contribution.

When women are undermined, their children become weak as well. In this way, a whole generation loses its strength and vitality. Only when women are accorded the honour they deserve, can we create a world of light and awareness.

Women can perform all tasks just as well as men—perhaps even better. Women have the willpower and creative energy to do any type of work. Amma can say this based on Her own experience. Whatever the form of action, women can attain extraordinary heights, and this is true especially on the spiritual path. Women have the purity of mind and intellectual capacity to achieve this. But, whatever they undertake, the beginning should be positive. If the beginning is good, the middle and the end will automatically be good, provided one has patience, faith, and love. A wrong beginning set on a faulty foundation is one of the reasons why women lose out so much in life. It isn't only that women should share equal status with men in society; the problem is that women are given a bad start in life, due to wrong understanding and lack of proper awareness. So, women are trying to reach the end without the benefit of having the beginning.

If we want to learn to read the Roman alphabet, we have to begin with ABC, not with XYZ. And what is the ABC of women? What is the very fibre of a woman's being, her existence? It is her inborn qualities, the essential principles of motherhood. Whatever area of work a woman chooses, she shouldn't forget these virtues that God or Nature has graciously bestowed on her. A woman should perform all her actions being firmly rooted in the very ground of these qualities. Just as ABC is the beginning of the alphabet, the quality of motherhood is the foundation of a woman. She shouldn't leave out that crucial part of herself before she moves on to other levels.

There are many powers in women that are generally not found in men. A woman has the ability to divide herself into many. Contrary to men, women have the capacity to do several things at the same time. Even if she has to divide herself, and do many different things simultaneously, a woman is gifted with the ability to carry out all actions with great beauty and perfection. Even in her role as a mother, a woman is able to bring forth many different facets of her being—she has to be warm and tender, strong and protective, and a strict disciplinarian. Rarely do we see this kind of confluence of qualities in men. So, in fact, women have a greater responsibility than men. Women hold the reins of integrity and unity in the family and in society.

A man's mind easily becomes identified with his thoughts and actions. Masculine energy can be compared to stagnant water; it doesn't flow. The mind and intellect of a man usually get stuck in the work that he does. It is difficult for men to shift their minds from one focus to another.

Because of this, the professional life and family life of many men become mixed up. Most men cannot separate the two. Women, on the other hand, have an inborn capacity to do this. It is a deep-rooted tendency of a man to bring his professional persona home and behave accordingly in his relationship with his wife and children. Most women know how to keep their family life and professional life separate.

Feminine energy, or a woman's energy, is fluid like a river. This makes it easy for a woman to be a mother, a wife, and a good friend who provides her husband with confidence. She has the special gift to be the guide and advisor of the entire family. Women who have jobs are more than capable of succeeding in that as well.

The power of a woman's innate motherhood helps her to find a deep sense of peace and harmony within herself. This enables her to reflect and react at the same time; whereas a man tends to reflect less and react more. A woman can listen to the sorrows of other people and respond with compassion; but, still, when faced with a challenge, she can rise to the situation and react as strongly as any man.

In today's world, everything is being contaminated and made unnatural. In this environment, woman should take extra care that her qualities of motherhood—her essential nature as a woman—don't become contaminated and distorted.

There is a man in the inner depths of every woman, and a woman in the inner depths of every man. This truth dawned in the meditation of the great saints and seers eons ago. This is what the Ardhanariswara (half God and half Goddess) concept in the Hindu faith signifies. Whether you are a woman or a man, your real humanity will come to light only when the feminine and masculine qualities within you are balanced.

Men have also suffered greatly as a result of the exile of the feminine principle from the world. Because of the oppression of women and the suppression of the feminine aspect within men, men's lives have become fragmented, often painful. Men, too, have to awaken to their feminine qualities. They have to develop empathy and understanding in their attitude towards women, and in the way they relate to the world.

Statistics show that men—not women—commit by far most of the crime and murder in this world. There is also a deep connection between the way men destroy Mother Nature and their attitude towards women. Nature should be accorded the same importance in our hearts as our own biological mothers.

Only love, compassion, and patience—the fundamental qualities of women—can lessen the intrinsically aggressive, overactive tendencies of men. Similarly, there are women who need the qualities of men, so that their good and gentle nature doesn't immobilize them.

Women are the power and the very foundation of our existence in the world. When women lose touch with their real selves, the harmony of the world ceases to exist, and destruction sets in. It is therefore crucial that women everywhere make every effort to rediscover their fundamental nature, for only then can we save this world.

What today's world really needs is cooperation between men and women, based on a firm sense of unity in the family and society. Wars and conflicts, all the suffering and lack of peace in the present-day world, will certainly lessen to a great extent if women and men begin to cooperate and to support each other. Unless harmony is restored between the masculine and the feminine, between men and women, peace will continue to be no more than a distant dream.

There are two types of language in the world: the language of the intellect and the language of the heart. The language of the dry, rational intellect likes to argue and attack. Aggression is its nature. It is purely masculine, devoid of love or any sense of relatedness. It says, "Not only am I right and you are wrong, but I have to prove this at all costs so that you will yield to me." Controlling others and making them puppets that dance according to their tune is typical of those who speak this language. They try to force their ideas on others. Their hearts are closed. They rarely consider anyone else's feelings. Their only consideration is their own ego and their hollow idea of victory.

The language of the heart, the language of love, which is related to the feminine principle, is quite different. Those who speak this language do not care about their ego. They have no interest in proving that they are right or that anyone else is wrong. They are deeply concerned about their fellow beings and wish to help, support, and uplift others. In their presence transformation simply happens. They are the givers of tangible hope and of light in this world. Those who approach them are reborn. When such people speak it is not to lecture, to impress or to argue—it is a true communion of hearts.

Real love has nothing to do with lust or self-centredness. In real love, you are not important; the other is important. In love, the other is not your instrument to fulfil your selfish desires; you are an instrument of the Divine with the intention of doing good in the world. Love does not sacrifice others; love gives joyfully of itself. Love is selfless—but not the enforced selflessness of women being pushed into the background, treated as objects. In real love, you do not feel worthless; on the contrary, you expand and become one with everything—all-encompassing, ever blissful.

Unfortunately, in today's world, it is the language of the intellect that prevails, not the language of the heart. Selfishness and the eyes of lust—not love—dominate the world. Narrow-minded people influence those with weaker minds and use them to fulfil their selfish goals. The ancient teachings of the sages have been distorted to fit within the narrow frames of men's selfish desires. The concept of love has been distorted. This is why the world is filled with conflicts, violence, and war.

Woman is the creator of the human race. She is the first Guru, the first guide and mentor of humanity. Think of the tremendous forces, either positive or negative, that one human being can unleash upon the world. Each one of us has a far-reaching effect on others, whether we are aware of it or not. The responsibility of a mother, when it comes to influencing and inspiring her children, cannot be underestimated. There is much truth in the saying that there is a strong woman behind every successful man. Wherever you see happy, peaceful individuals; wherever you see children endowed with noble qualities and good dispositions; wherever you see men who have immense strength when faced with failure and adverse situations; wherever you see people who possess a great measure of understanding, sympathy, love, and compassion towards the suffering, and who give of themselves to others—you will usually find a great mother who has inspired them to become what they are.

Mothers are the ones who are most able to sow the seeds of love, universal kinship, and patience in the minds of human beings. There is a special bond between a mother and child. The mother's inner qualities are transmitted to the child even through her breast milk. The mother understands the heart of her child; she pours her love into the child, teaches him or her the positive lessons of life, and corrects the child's mistakes. If you walk through a field of soft, green grass a few times, you will easily make a path. The good thoughts and positive values we cultivate in our children will stay with them forever. It is easy to mould a child's character when he or she is very young, and much more difficult to do so when the child grows up.

Once, when Amma was giving darshan in India, a youth came up to her. He lived in a part of the country that was ravaged by terrorism. Because of the frequent killings and lootings, the people in that area were suffering a great deal. He told Amma that he was the leader of a group of youngsters who were doing a lot of social work in that area. He prayed to Amma, "Please give those terrorists, who are so full of hatred and violence, the right understanding. And for all those who have faced so many atrocities and have suffered so much, please fill their hearts with the spirit of forgiveness. Otherwise, the situation will only deteriorate, and there will be no end to the violence."

Amma was so glad to hear his prayer for peace and forgiveness. When Amma asked him what made him choose a life of social work, he said, "My mother was the inspiration behind this. My childhood days were dark and terrifying. When I was six years old, I watched with my own eyes as my peace-loving father was brutally murdered by terrorists. My life was shattered. I was filled with hatred, and all I wanted was revenge. But my mother changed my attitude. Whenever I would tell her that I was going to avenge my father's death one day, she would say, 'Son, will your father come back to life if you kill those people? Look at your grandmother, how sad she always is. Look at me, how difficult it is to make both ends meet without your father. And just look at yourself, how sad you are, not having your father with you. Would you want more mothers and children to suffer as we do? The intensity of this pain would be the same for them. Try to forgive your father's killers for their terrible deeds, and spread the message of love and universal kinship instead.' When I grew up, people tried to get me to join different terrorist outfits to avenge my father's death. But the seeds of forgiveness sown by my mother had borne fruit, and I refused. I gave some of the youngsters the same advice that my mother had given me. This changed the hearts of many people who have since joined me in serving others."

The love and compassion, rather than hatred, that this boy chose to pour into the world, stemmed from the wellspring of love in his mother.

It is thus, through the influence she has on her child, that a mother influences the future of the world. A woman who has awakened her innate motherhood brings heaven to earth wherever she is. Only women can create a peaceful, happy world. And so it is that the one who rocks the cradle of the babe is the one who holds up the lamp, shedding light upon the world.

Men should never hinder a woman's progress towards her rightful position in society. They should understand that the full contribution of women to the world is vitally important. Men should move out of her path; nay, they should prepare her path, to make her forward movement smoother.

A woman, for her part, should think of what she can give to society, rather than what she can take. This attitude will certainly help her to progress. It should be underscored that a woman doesn't need to receive or to take anything from anyone. She simply needs to awaken. Then she will be able to contribute whatever she wishes to give to society, and she will gain everything she needs.

Rather than becoming rusty, living out their lives inside the four walls of the kitchen, women should come out and share with others what they have to give, and fulfil their goals in life. Today, when competition and anger are the norm everywhere, it is the patience and tolerance of women that create whatever harmony there is in the world. Just as a complete electrical circuit depends on the presence of both positive and negative poles, life flowing in all its fullness depends on the presence and contribution of women as well as of men. Only when women and men complement and support each other will their inner blossoming take place.

In general, today's women are living in a world fashioned by and for men. Women have no need of that world; they should establish their own identities, and thus recreate society. But they should remember the real meaning of freedom. It is not a license to live and behave any way one likes, regardless of the consequences for others; it doesn't mean that wives and mothers should run away from their family responsibilities. A woman's freedom and rising has to begin within herself. Also, for *shakti*, or pure power, to awaken and arise in a woman, she first has to become aware of her weaknesses. She can then overcome those weaknesses through her willpower, selfless service, and spiritual practice.

In the process of striving to regain their rightful position in society, women should never lose their essential nature. This tendency can be seen in many countries, and will never help women to achieve true freedom. It is impossible to attain real freedom by imitating men. If women themselves turn their backs on the feminine principle, this will culminate in the utter failure of women and society. Then the problems of the world will not be resolved, but only aggravated. If women reject their feminine qualities and try to become like men, cultivating only masculine qualities, the imbalance in the world will only become greater. This is not the need of the age. The real need is for women to contribute all they can to society by developing their universal motherhood, as well as their masculine qualities.

As long as women do not make the effort to awaken, they are, in a way, themselves responsible for creating their own narrow world.

The more a woman identifies with her inner motherhood, the more she awakens to that *shakti*, or pure power. When women develop this power within themselves, the world will begin to listen to their voices more and more.

Many commendable individuals and organizations, like the UN, are supporting the progress of women. This conference is an opportunity for us to build on that foundation. Amma would like to share a few suggestions.

1. Religious leaders should make every effort to guide their followers back to the true essence of spirituality, and in light of this, condemn all types of oppression and violence against women.

2. The UN should go in and provide safe havens for women and children in war zones and areas of communal strife where they are particularly targeted.

3. All religions and nations should condemn such

shameful practices as female foeticide and infanticide, and female genital mutilation.

4. Child labour should be stopped.

5. The dowry system should be abolished.

6. The UN and leaders of every nation should intensify their efforts to stop child trafficking and the sexual exploitation of young girls. The legal consequences of such behaviour should be effective deterrents.

7. The number of rapes taking place all over the world is astounding. And the fact that in some countries it is the *victims* of rape who are punished is incomprehensible. Can we merely stand by and watch this?

There should be a concerted, international effort to educate young men, with the aim of putting an end to rape and other forms of violence against women.

8. The dignity of women is assailed by advertisements that treat them as sex objects. We should not tolerate this exploitation.

9. Religious leaders should encourage their followers to make selfless service an integral part of their lives.

The essence of motherhood is not restricted to women who have given birth; it is a principle inherent in both women and men. It is an attitude of the mind. It is love—and that love is the very breath of life. No one would say, "I will breathe only when I am with my family and friends; I won't breathe in front of my enemies." Similarly, for those in whom motherhood has awakened, love and compassion for everyone is as much part of their being as breathing.

Amma feels that the forthcoming age should be dedicated to reawakening the healing power of motherhood. This is the only way to realize our dream of peace and harmony for all. And it can be done! It is entirely up to us. Let us remember this and move forward.

Amma would like to thank all those involved in organizing this summit. Amma deeply honours your efforts to bring peace to this world. May the seeds of peace we are planting here today bear fruit for all.

Aum Namah Shivaya

Universal Motherhood

Book Catalog
By Author

Sri Mata Amritanandamayi Devi
108 Quotes On Faith
108 Quotes On Love
Compassion, The Only Way To Peace: Paris Speech
Cultivating Strength And Vitality
Living In Harmony
May Peace And Happiness Prevail: Barcelona Speech
May Your Hearts Blossom: Chicago Speech
Practice Spiritual Values And Save The World: Delhi Speech
The Awakening Of Universal Motherhood: Geneva Speech
The Eternal Truth
The Infinite Potential Of Women: Jaipur Speech
Understanding And Collaboration Between Religions
Unity Is Peace: Interfaith Speech

Swami Amritaswarupananda Puri
Ammachi: A Biography
Awaken Children, Volumes 1-9
From Amma's Heart
Mother Of Sweet Bliss
The Color Of Rainbow

Swami Jnanamritananda Puri
Eternal Wisdom, Volumes 1-2

Swami Paramatmananda Puri
On The Road To Freedom Volumes 1-2
Talks, Volumes 1-6

Swami Purnamritananda Puri
Unforgettable Memories

Swami Ramakrishnananda Puri
Eye Of Wisdom
Racing Along The Razor's Edge
Secret Of Inner Peace
The Blessed Life
The Timeless Path
Ultimate Success

Swamini Krishnamrita Prana
Love Is The Answer
Sacred Journey
The Fragrance Of Pure Love
Torrential Love

M.A. Center Publications
1,000 Names Commentary
Archana Book (Large)
Archana Book (Small)
Being With Amma
Bhagavad Gita
Bhajanamritam, Volumes 1-6
Embracing The World
For My Children
Immortal Light
Lead Us To Purity
Lead Us To The Light
Man And Nature
My First Darshan
Puja: The Process Of Ritualistic Worship
Sri Lalitha Trishati Stotram

Amma's Websites

AMRITAPURI—Amma's Home Page
Teachings, Activities, Ashram Life, eServices, Yatra, Blogs and News
http://www.amritapuri.org

AMMA (Mata Amritanandamayi)
About Amma, Meeting Amma, Global Charities, Groups and Activities and Teachings
http://www.amma.org

EMBRACING THE WORLD®
Basic Needs, Emergencies, Environment, Research and News
http://www.embracingtheworld.org

AMRITA UNIVERSITY
About, Admissions, Campuses, Academics, Research, Global and News
http://www.amrita.edu

THE AMMA SHOP—Embracing the World® Books & Gifts Shop
Blog, Books, Complete Body, Home & Gifts, Jewelry, Music and Worship
http://www.theammashop.org

IAM—Integrated Amrita Meditation Technique®
Meditation Taught Free of Charge to the Public, Students, Prisoners and Military
http://www.amma.org/groups/north-america/projects/iam-meditation-classes

AMRITA PUJA
Types and Benefits of Pujas, Brahmasthanam Temple, Astrology Readings, Ordering Pujas
http://www.amritapuja.org

GREENFRIENDS
Growing Plants, Building Sustainable Environments, Education and Community Building
http://www.amma.org/groups/north-america/projects/green-friends

FACEBOOK
This is the Official Facebook Page to Connect with Amma
https://www.facebook.com/MataAmritanandamayi

DONATION PAGE
Please Help Support Amma's Charities Here:
http://www.amma.org/donations

www.ingramcontent.com/pod-product-compliance
Lightning Source LLC
Chambersburg PA
CBHW071316060426
42444CB00036B/3068